Presented to

_____

On the occasion of

_____

From

_____

Date

_____

All Scripture quotations marked (NIV) are taken from the HOLY BIBLE, NEW INTERNATIONAL VERSION® NIV®. Copyright© 1973, 1978, 1984 by International Bible Society. Used by permission of Zondervan Publishing House. All rights reserved.

Scripture quotations marked (NLT) are taken from the HOLY BIBLE, New Living Translation. Copyright© 1996. Used by permission of Tyndale House Publishers, Inc., Wheaton, Illinois 60189. All right reserved.

Scripture quotations marked (TLB) are taken from THE LIVING BIBLE, Copyright© 1971. Used by permission of Tyndale House Publishers, Inc., Wheaton, Illinois 60189. All rights reserved.

All Scripture quotations marked (KJV) are taken from the Authorized King James Version of the Bible.

Other acknowledgments:
Pages 5, 19, 28, 30, 36, 39—from *Legacy of Joy: A Devotional for Fathers,* published by Promise Press (1998); page 8—used by permission of Donna Lange; page 11—used by permission of Sheila Stewart; page 26—from *He Cares for You,* published by Fleming H. Revell (1998).

Published by Barbour Publishing, Inc., P.O. Box 719, Uhrichsville, Ohio 44683
http://www.barbourbooks.com

Member of the
Evangelical Christian
Publishers Association

Printed in China.

A STRONG HAND TO HOLD

A CELEBRATION OF FATHERHOOD

Compiled by
Ben Preston

BARBOUR
PUBLISHING, INC.

THE VOCATION OF FATHERHOOD

That our sons may be as plants grown up in their youth; that our daughters may be as corner stones, polished after the similitude of a palace. . . yea, happy is that people, whose God is the LORD.

—PSALM 144:12, 15 (KJV)

There is no more vital calling or vocation
for men than fathering.

—JOHN THROOP, *Parents and Children*

Most of us are proud to be dads. But sometimes life is just so busy. We forget how very important our vocation is. We take our children for granted.

4

HOMEBLIND

How could you be blind to something you look at a dozen times or more a day?

Scientists call it being "homeblind." Commonplace details fail to register. . . . You are "homeblind" to the familiar. And sometimes we fathers become homeblind to the precious joy our children provide and possess.

Remember how you felt the first time you held your infant child? Remember the miracle? The rush of relief and joyful exhilaration?

You still hold that precious child, only now that child can hold you back. Don't be blind to the joy that brings.

—MIKE NAPPA AND NORM WAKEFIELD
Legacy of Joy: A Devotional for Fathers

Let us look upon our children,
let us love them and train them,
as children of the covenant and
children of the promise—
these are the children of God.

—ANDREW MURRAY
How to Raise Your Children for Christ

Finally, brothers, whatever is true, whatever is noble, whatever is right, whatever is pure, whatever is lovely, whatever is admirable— if anything is excellent or praiseworthy—think about such things.

—PAUL (PHILIPPIANS 4:8, NIV)

CATCHING GOD'S REFLECTION IN OUR MIRROR

And we, who with unveiled faces all reflect the Lord's glory, are being transformed into his likeness.

—PAUL (2 CORINTHIANS 3:18, NIV)

A child identifies his parents with God, whether the adults want that role or not. Most children "see" God the way they perceive their earthly fathers.

—JAMES DOBSON, *The Strong-Willed Child*

Bearing God's image is a big responsibility. We need to be careful to make the most of this awesome opportunity. This doesn't mean we have to have long, theological discussions with our children. Sometimes, all it means is that we take the time to surprise our kids with "treasures," little delights embedded in ordinary life that will teach our children far more about God's nature than any religious sermon.

HIDDEN TREASURE

"Jonathan, please go outside and play. You can look for treasure," his mom suggested.

Jonathan ran out the kitchen door. He picked up sticks and inspected their shapes. He peered into the crevices of the rock wall that bordered the backyard. He turned over a pile of bricks. "Just slugs," he muttered to himself. As he rounded the corner of the garage, he bent over and stared. Slowly he fingered a rough texture. He tried to pick it up, but it did not budge.

"You won't believe it! I found a smiley-face rock!" Jonathan shouted as he rushed into the house.

"Is it shaped like a circle?" his dad asked.

"Did you see it?" Jonathan asked.

"Show me," his dad said.

The family walked between the woodpile and the garage. Jonathan knelt by the pitted face. He rubbed the deep indentations for eyes, the stone nose, and the curved line for a smile.

His dad smiled.

"How did this get here?" his mom asked his dad.

"I made it the other day from leftover cement. I wanted to see how long it would take Jonathan to find it. It really isn't a big thing."

"Sure it is," his mom answered. "It's hidden treasure."

8

Hidden treasure. It strengthened the father's relationship with his son. It can also strengthen a child's relationship with his heavenly Father. How do we teach our children to find God's hidden treasures?

First, we need to encourage our children to search. Hidden treasure is not obvious. It takes work to find it. We need to show our children how to persist when searching for an answer, even if disappointed. Just like explorers on an expedition, we need to equip our children with a map. The map for life is God's Word. By memorizing Scripture, God's Word is hidden in their hearts. They are equipped to hear God "cheer them on," just as we parents root for our kids at Little League games and soccer practice.

The joy doesn't end once you've discovered your treasure. Just like Jonathan finding his smiley rock, he shared the prize with someone important to him. We should listen to our children when they want to share a truth they've learned from God.

Leftover cement created into a smiley face. The simple act cost very little time and money. The reward was great. The smiley-face rock will remain for years, a tangible reminder of a father's love. It is also a reflection of God's love and interest in His children.

What kind of image of God do our children see when they look at us? Are we planting hidden treasures in our children's lives?

—DONNA LANGE

If we as parents are too busy to
listen to our children,
how then can they understand
a God who hears?

—V. GILBERT BEERS
How to Raise Christian Kids in a Non-Christian World

Can't you see the Creator of the universe, who understands every
secret, every mystery, sitting patiently and listening to a four-
year-old talk to him? That's a beautiful image of a father.

—JAMES DOBSON

A Daughter's Perspective

I have a memory, from when I was about three years old, of riding on my father's shoulders. I had his hair wrapped around my fingers, and he had a firm grip on my legs. The thought of falling didn't even occur to me: He was my Daddy. He was praying out loud, I remember, and I was worried that might mean he would have to close his eyes. Even Daddy might walk into something if he had his eyes shut. "No," he said. "God can always hear us. Even with our eyes open."

That's one of my earliest memories of my father. The sun shone and everything was good; my Daddy was wonderful.

Memories like that send a dizzying rush of love through me—what people call "warm-fuzzies," but too strong and real to be labeled so simplistically. I wish I could say that things were always as good between my father and me, but the truth is, I was a brat. I did my worst rebelling before I turned five, but unfortunately the tendency continued to crop up from time to time after that. I threw temper tantrums in public places and waged war at nearly every meal, refusing to eat all but a select menu. Memories like that shame my recollections of the child I once was.

It's interesting to me that in the good memories, my father was actively wonderful, while I was simply the recipient, calmed by him, enjoying him. On the other hand, in the less-than-good memories, I'm the one who was actively terrible, while my father simply tried to deal with me. He punished me when I pushed the issue, but I was the one who brought the punishment on myself.

I suppose my growing up years must have been like an extended infancy in my relationship with God. That's why now, as I develop as an adult, I seem to be at the same place with God that I was at with my father twenty years ago. In a way, that makes me nervous: Dad and I have had a lot of disagreements over the years, and we still do occasionally. But I consider him a friend, and that overwhelming love I had for him as a small child I still have for him today.

God is the greatest, most wonderful Father in the universe, and my father's love is only the tiniest echo of His. I want God to be my friend, and He is—but He is also my parent. That's why I know I can look forward to trials, as He cleans out my nasty corners. But I'm also looking forward to an ever-deepening relationship with Him, as I get to know Him better and become more like Him.

—SHEILA STEWART

The voice of parents is
the voice of God's,
for to their children,
they are heaven's lieutenants.

—WILLIAM SHAKESPEARE

LITTLE PEOPLE WHO WAKE US UP

Let the little children come to me, and do not hinder them, for the kingdom of God belongs to such as these. I tell you the truth, anyone who will not receive the kingdom of God like a little child will never enter it.

—JESUS (MARK 10:14–15, NIV)

There is so much that is beautiful and good to wake up to. Our children drive us toward this awakening.

—POLLY BERRIEN BERENDS, *Whole Child/Whole Parent*

I wonder if we who have grown up will ever know on this side of the grave how much we owe to children, who seem, but only seem, to owe us so much.

—FRANCIS C. KELLEY

The soul is healed by being with children.

—Fyodor Dostoevsky

A world without children is
a world without newness,
regeneration, color, and vigor.

—James Dobson

Sometimes—especially on a Saturday morning—we don't feel like being woken up by our children. We're tired and we're busy, and we're understandably a little grouchy sometimes. Besides, it's pretty humbling to realize all that we can learn from our children. We may have more knowledge, experience, and physical strength than they do, but they have an openness that allows them to see God more clearly than we can sometimes. They are never too busy, too worried, too preoccupied with the day's stresses. As fathers we are blessed with the chance to share a child's world, and re-experience the wonder they feel for God and His creation.

14

Like a Little Child

[Jesus] never talked to children about what they could learn from adults, but He did tell adults some things to learn from children! How contrary to the thinking of that day, which held that adults were wise and children lacked wisdom. Since children were to learn from adults, how could adults learn from children? How shocking, then, that Jesus reversed this view!

Want to enter God's kingdom?
Then become like little children.
Want to be great in God's eyes?
Then become like little children.
Want to let Jesus know you welcome and receive him?
Then welcome little children.

—ROY ZUCK
Precious in His Sight

Children think not of what is past, nor what is to come, but enjoy the present time, which few of us do.

—JEAN DE LA BRUYERE

The parents exist to teach the child, but also they must learn what the child has to teach them; and the child has a very great deal to teach.

—ARNOLD BENNETT

A parent must respect the spiritual person of his child, and approach it with reverence.

—GEORGE MACDONALD

And whoever welcomes a little child like this in my name welcomes me.

—JESUS (MATTHEW 18:5, NIV)

ASSEMBLY REQUIRED

Giving all diligence, add to your faith virtue; and to virtue knowledge; And to knowledge temperance; and to temperance patience; and to patience godliness; And to godliness brotherly kindness; and to brotherly kindness charity. For if these things be in you, and abound, they make you that ye shall neither be barren nor unfruitful.

—2 PETER 1: 5–8 (KJV)

The difficult thing about children is that
they come with no instructions.
You pretty well have to
assemble them on your own.

—JAMES DOBSON

Making babies may be an innate skill, but being a competent father is not. It is learned. . . . If we dads are going to make it, we have to give the same diligence to fathering that it takes to be competent as a plumber, pilot, or any other professional.

—PAUL LEWIS, from *Christian Parenting Today*

Most of us probably never realized just how hard being a dad was going to be. We probably pictured ourselves throwing a ball in the backyard, sharing the things we used to enjoy as a kid—but we most likely didn't anticipate the times when our children would demand more of us than we felt we could conveniently give, the times they would challenge us in ways that weren't easy to accept. There's no way around it: raising kids is hard work sometimes—and it takes time. We have to make a definite commitment to our children, giving them not only our love, but our time.

YOUR WORK WILL
ALWAYS BE THERE

All of [the] statistics about fathers boil down to time. Your absence from your family—physical, emotional, or spiritual—hinders your ability to transfer joy to your children. Likewise, when you buck the trend and commit to simply being there for your kids, you lay a foundation on which joy can be built.

You will always have work; you won't always have preschoolers, or elementary kids, or junior high and high schoolers running in and out of your doors. Make the choice to spend enough time with your kids that your wife would respond with an enthusiastic "Yes!" to the question "Do your children and their father often do things together?"

—MIKE NAPPA AND NORM WAKEFIELD
Legacy of Joy: A Devotional for Fathers

A STRONG HAND TO HOLD

Children just don't fit into a "to do" list very well. It takes time to be an effective parent when children are small. It takes time to introduce them to good books—it takes time to fly kites and play punch ball and put together jigsaw puzzles. It takes time to listen.

—JAMES DOBSON

Have you taken time lately to thank God for these wonderful gifts you call your children? Or has life been so busy that you see them only as challenges, as mischiefs, as time-eaters, as heavy responsibilities, or as headaches and problems?

—TIM HANSEL, *What Kids Need Most in a Dad*

When we love something it is of value to us, and when something is of value to us we spend time with it, time enjoying it and time taking care of it. . . . So it is when we love children; we spend time admiring them and caring for them. We give them our time.

—M. SCOTT PECK, *The Road Less Traveled*

Whatever you do,
work at it with all your heart,
as working for the Lord, not for men,
since you know that you will receive
an inheritance from the Lord as a reward.

—COLOSSIANS 3:23–24 (NIV)

PATIENCE

Fathers, do not exasperate your children; instead, bring them up in the training and instruction of the Lord.

—PAUL (EPHESIANS 6:4, NIV)

Some parents bring up their children on thunder and lightning, but thunder and lightning never yet made anything grow. Rain or sunshine cause growth—quiet penetrating forces that develop life.

—UNKNOWN

To be patient in little things, to be tolerant in large affairs, to be happy in the midst of petty cares and monotonies, that is wisdom.

—JOSEPH FORT NEWTON

No doubt about it, raising kids takes lots of patience. You might say patience is the cornerstone of a father's vocation. Or your could say it's the glue that holds the whole thing together. Not only that, however, our patience is the thing that will open eternity's door for our kids.

Combine Mercy with Loving Discipline

If parents behave lovingly toward their children, combining mercy with loving discipline, and loving discipline with fatherly and motherly compassion, they are more likely to save their children's hearts than if they were stern and short-tempered. Our children must still make their own eternal decisions for themselves—but at least we will know, whatever they should choose, that in love we have done all that we could to keep our children safe.

—John Bunyan, *The Riches of Bunyan*

A STRONG HAND TO HOLD

A man can do only what he can do.
But if he does that each day
he can sleep at night
and do it again the next day.

—ALBERT SCHWEITZER

Love is active and sincere;
courageous, patient, faithful,
prudent, and manly.

—THOMAS À KEMPIS

And we urge you, brothers, . . .encourage the timid, help the weak, be patient with everyone.

—1 THESSALONIANS 5:14 (NIV)

SPITTING IMAGES

A man finds out what is meant by
a spitting image when he
tries to feed cereal to his infant.

Children seldom misquote you.
They more often repeat word for word
what you shouldn't have said.

Children are truly "spitting images": they mirror our own behavior, for good or bad. Whatever habits of ours they observe, will probably one day be their own. As much as possible, let's make sure they observe good habits that will lead them into a lifetime of Christian discipline.

A Father Who Prayed

My father prayed because he had a good Friend with whom to share the problems of the day. He prayed because he had a direct connection with his Maker when he had a concern. He prayed because there was so much for which he was thankful.

...When I was a little girl I was sure that Jesus was a member of the ten Boom family. It was just as easy to talk to Him as it was to carry on a conversation with my mother and father. Jesus was there. I was closer to the reality and truth of Jesus' presence than the one who makes fellowship with the Lord a problem by reasoning and logical thinking.

—CORRIE TEN BOOM, *He Cares for You*

If you want your child to
walk the righteous path,
do not merely point the way—
lead the way.

—J.A. ROSENKRANZ

Religious words have value
to the child only as experience
in the home gives them meaning.

—JOHN DRESCHER

YOU ONLY GET
ONE CHANCE

Philip Yancey, in his wonderful book, *What's So Amazing About Grace*, tells a brief story of a friend of his named George. . . . George's marriage had gone through angry, difficult times. Finally one night, George reached his breaking point, pounded the table and the floor, and screamed, "I hate you!" at his wife. "I won't take it anymore! I've had enough! I won't go on! I won't let it happen! No! No! No!"

The couple managed to stay together, working to repair the broken relationship. Then, months later, George was awakened by noises from the bedroom of their two-year-old son. George listened at his son's door, and shivers ran through his flesh. In a soft voice, the two-year-old was repeating word for word with precise inflection, "I hate you! . . . I won't take it anymore! . . . No! No! No!"

Yancey writes, "George realized that in some awful way he had just bequeathed his pain and anger and unforgiveness to the next generation."

Your child only gets one childhood. You can fill it with shrieks of laughter and tickles or cries of anger and pain. Which will you choose?

—MIKE NAPPA AND NORM WAKEFIELD
Legacy of Joy: A Devotional for Fathers

Children are very nice observers,
and will often perceive your slightest defect.

—FRANCIS DE SALES FENELON

Children are natural mimics—
they act like their parents in spite of
every attempt to teach them good manners.

—BOB KELLY

The best way to train up a child
the way he should go,
is to travel that road occasionally yourself.

—JOSH BILLINGS

As Ye Sow, So Shall Ye Reap

Most of us cherish memories of sitting on a parent's lap and hearing a favorite story. . . .

One favorite is from the Brothers Grimm. "The Old Grandfather's Table" involves a frail old man who went to live with his son, daughter-in-law, and four-year-old grandson. The old man's hands trembled, his eyesight was blurred, and his step faltered.

The family ate together at the table. But the elderly grandfather's shaky hands and failing sight made eating difficult. Peas rolled off his spoon onto the floor. When he grasped the glass, milk spilled on the tablecloth. The son and daughter-in-law became irritated with the mess.

"We must do something about Grandfather," said the son. "I've had enough of his spilled milk, noisy eating, and food on the floor."

So the husband and wife set a small table in the corner. There Grandfather ate alone while the rest of the family enjoyed dinner. Since Grandfather had broken a dish or two, his food was served in a wooden bowl. When the family glanced in Grandfather's direction, sometimes he had a tear in his eye as he sat alone. Still, the only words the couple had for him were sharp admonitions when he dropped a fork or spilled food.

The four-year-old watched it all in silence.

One evening before supper, the father noticed his son playing with wood scraps on the floor. He asked the child sweetly, "What are you making?"

Just as sweetly the boy responded, "Oh, I'm making a little bowl for Papa and Mama to eat their food in when I grow up." The four-year-old smiled and went back to work. The words so struck the parents that they were speechless. Then tears started to stream down their cheeks. Though no word was spoken, both knew what must be done.

That evening the husband took Grandfather's hand and gently led him back to the family table. For the remainder of his days he ate every meal with the family. And for some reason, neither husband nor wife seemed to care any longer when a fork was dropped, milk spilled, or the tablecloth soiled.

Children are remarkably perceptive. Their eyes ever observe, their ears ever listen, and their minds ever process the messages they absorb. If they see us patiently provide a happy home atmosphere for our family members, they will imitate that attitude for the rest of their lives. The wise parent realizes that every day the building blocks are being laid for the child's future. Let's be wise builders.

—MIKE NAPPA AND NORM WAKEFIELD
Legacy of Joy: A Devotional for Fathers

The words a father speaks to his children in the privacy of the home are not overheard at the time, but as in whispering galleries, they will be heard at the end and by posterity.

—JEAN PAUL RICHTER

Parents who expect their children
to follow in their footsteps
should be careful about
dragging their feet.

—REV. GEORGE HALL

Only be careful, and watch yourselves closely so that you do not forget the things your eyes have seen or let them slip from your heart as long as you live. Teach them to your children and to their children after them.

—MOSES (DEUTERONOMY 4:9, NIV)

LOVE THEM AND
LOSE THEM

Commit your work to the Lord,
then it will succeed.

—PROVERBS 16:3 (TLB)

Children make parents grow up a lot more than parents make children grow up. . . . Your child is going to walk away from you. In one respect it requires more generosity to dedicate yourself to someone who will walk away. Your child is by definition unresponsive, unthankful.

—JAMES BURTCHAELL

It takes courage to let our children go, but we are trustees and stewards and have to hand them back to life—to God. As the old saying puts it: "What I gave I have." We have to love them and lose them.

True parenthood is self-destructive. The wise parent is one who effectively does himself out of his job as parent. The silver cord must be broken. It must not be broken too abruptly, but it must be broken. The child must cease to be a child. . . .

—ROBERT HOLMES

When our kids are small, we feel as though the day will never come when we won't be bruising our bare feet on Legos, tripping over stuffed animals, or hearing the crunch of another broken crayon beneath our shoes. And then suddenly we realize we no longer have a toddler in the house. And then we no longer have a grade-school child. And one day they're gone.

It's hard to let go. None of us like to face pain of any sort. But with God's help, we can praise Him even when the house echoes with emptiness and our hands long for those little fingers that once clutched ours.

KIDS AT HEART

I tell you the truth, unless you change and become like little children, you will never enter the kingdom of heaven.

—JESUS (MATTHEW 18:3, NIV)

If a child is to keep alive his inborn sense of wonder, he needs the companionship of at least one adult who can share it, rediscovering with him the joy, excitement and mystery of the world we live in.

—RACHEL CARSON

One of the best parts of being a dad is that it means you never really have to grow up all the way. You can still rough house and goof around and act foolish; in fact, the more you do it, the more your kids giggle. What a great deal: you get to show off like a ten-year-old, and you have a non-stop, appreciative audience for every silly thing you do.

But guess what? Even the fun, silly times can help your children grow closer to their heavenly Father.

PLAYMATES

"Okay, I'll admit it," says Mike. "When my wife asked our four-year-old son what he liked best about Dad, I half-hoped he'd shout, 'He's the smartest dad in the world!' Or better, 'He's the strongest dad alive!'

"Instead, Tony gave a greater compliment. 'I like best about my dad,' he said after a moment's thought, 'that he plays with me.'

"I had thought kneeling among his collection of toys was just another 'dad duty.' Now I realize it's a *privilege*. And I've discovered play can open doors for faith development and leave a legacy of joy."

So how can a father make the most of play? Here are a few suggestions:

Ignite the imagination using Scripture as the spark. David and Goliath is Tony's favorite Bible story, so for a birthday party we used homemade toys and played games with that story's theme. A dozen little ones were thrilled to fling toy slings toward a menacing "Goliath" target. We've used Bible action figures to play "What if . . . ?" What if Peter had faced Goliath? What if you and I were threatened by the fiery furnace instead of Shadrach, Meshach, and Abednego?

Keep it simple. Don't cover "The Four Spiritual Laws" each time you pull out a Christian toy. Don't feel compelled to discuss theology over Mary and Esther dolls. Avoid being preachy or complicated or inflexible. It's the relationship that earns trust, which allows you to speak at the right time about faith in Jesus.

Demonstrate enthusiasm. Whether it's playing a new CD-ROM game on the computer or dressing up in sheets to play "Joseph and Mary Go to Bethlehem," show by example that it's okay to have fun. Your actions tell your child that faith in Jesus is accompanied by joy.

Make play a priority. In Mike's house, after dinner is typically "family time." Everyone—parent and child alike—puts aside demands of the day and focuses on playing and hanging out together. Sometimes the family plays board games; other times they play with action figures or in the backyard. It really doesn't matter what happens, as long as there is a commitment to doing it.

"During those after-dinner times," says Mike, "I remember what I like best about my son. It's that he plays with me, too."

—MIKE NAPPA AND NORM WAKEFIELD
Legacy of Joy: A Devotional for Fathers

A HEAVENLY HERITAGE

*Sons are a heritage from the LORD,
children a reward from him.*

—SOLOMON (PSALM 127:3, NIV)

Our children are the only possessions
we can take to heaven.

—BOB KELLY

Our children are part of our eternal heritage. If we have raised them to know Christ, then one day we will spend forever praising God together. But children are not only a spiritual heritage. In very real and practical ways, through our children, we touch the future. The faith we pass along will continue to shape the world generations from now.

From Generation to Generation

Memories. . .become the foundation for the legacy your children inherit from you, and the impression points by which your children form their view of God, our heavenly Father. If your children remember that you were never available to them, your legacy is abandonment (whether you live with your kids or not). If your children remember you as someone who constantly criticized, your legacy will be dissatisfaction.

Imagine how your daughter's life will be different if, instead of remembering a frown on dad's face, she sees your smile. Think what changes might occur if your son remembers, not the hours you put in at the office, but the hours you spent playing with him.

By creating happy memories for your children, you create a legacy of joy to pass on from generation to generation.

—MIKE NAPPA AND NORM WAKEFIELD
Legacy of Joy: A Devotional for Fathers

THE LAST WILL
AND TESTAMENT
OF PATRICK HENRY

I have now disposed of all my property to my family. There is one thing more I wish I could give them and that is faith in Jesus Christ. If they had that and I had not given them one shilling, they would be rich; and if they had not that, and I had given them the world, they would be poor indeed.

As for me and my family,
we will serve the LORD.

—JOSHUA 24:15 (NLT)